Suffrage Sisters

The Fight for Liberty

Written by Maggie Mead

Illustrated by
Siri Weber Feeney

RED
CHAIR
·PRESS·

Please visit our website at **www.redchairpress.com** for more high-quality products for young readers.

 EDUCATORS: Find FREE lesson plans and a Readers' Theater script for
this book at www.redchairpress.com/free-activities.

About the Author

Maggie Mead has written numerous biographies, news articles, and plays. A former editor
of Weekly Reader's newsmagazine *Current Events*, she is currently assistant editor of Scholastic's
science periodical *SuperScience*.

Suffrage Sisters: The Fight for Liberty

Publisher's Cataloging-In-Publication Data
(Prepared by The Donohue Group, Inc.)

Mead, Margaret R.
Suffrage sisters : the fight for liberty / by Maggie Mead ; illustrated by Siri Weber Feeney.

pages : illustrations ; cm. -- (Setting the stage for fluency)

Summary: Demanding equal rights for women, including the right to vote, several generations of
courageous women devoted their lives to liberty and equality. This story is told by three brave women--
Elizabeth Cady Stanton, Susan B. Anthony, and Alice Paul--who fought in the women's suffrage fight.
Interest age level: 009-012.
Issued also as an ebook.
Includes bibliographical references.
ISBN: 978-1-939656-78-1 (library binding/hardcover)
ISBN: 978-1-939656-69-8 (paperback)

1. Stanton, Elizabeth Cady, 1815-1902--Juvenile drama. 2. Anthony, Susan B. (Susan Brownell),
1820-1906--Juvenile drama. 3. Paul, Alice, 1885-1977--Juvenile drama. 4. Suffragists--United States--
Biography--Juvenile drama. 5. Women--Suffrage--United States--History--Juvenile drama. 6. Women's
rights--United States--History--Juvenile drama. 7. Stanton, Elizabeth Cady, 1815-1902--Drama. 8. Anthony,
Susan B. (Susan Brownell), 1820-1906--Drama. 9. Paul, Alice, 1885-1977--Drama. 10. Suffragists--United
States--Biography--Drama. 11. Women--Suffrage--United States--History--Drama. 12. Women's rights--
United States--History--Drama. 13. Children's plays, American. 14. Historical drama. 15. Biographical
drama. I. Feeney, Siri Weber. II. Title.

PS3613.E24 S84 2015
[Fic]   2014944176

This series first published by:
Red Chair Press LLC   PO Box 333   South Egremont, MA 01258-0333

Printed in the United States of America

1 2 3 4 5 18 17 16 15 14

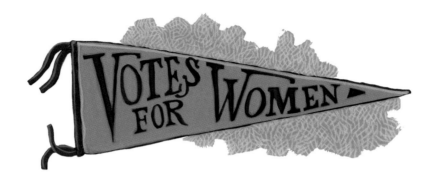

TABLE OF CONTENTS

INTRODUCTION

For much of American history, women were second-class citizens. They didn't have the same rights as men to own property. They couldn't work most jobs. They weren't allowed to attend most colleges. And, most importantly, they didn't have the right to vote.

In 1848, Elizabeth Cady Stanton gave a famous speech, called the Declaration of Sentiments. In it, she demanded the same rights as men. Women across the country soon joined Stanton and other leaders in the long struggle for women's suffrage, the right to vote. Generations later, Alice Paul led women in the final years of the suffrage fight. Her large, theatrical parades and protests finally led to the passage of the 19th Amendment in 1920.

This story is told by three brave women—Elizabeth Cady Stanton, Susan B. Anthony, and Alice Paul—at key moments in the women's suffrage fight. Each of these leaders had to make unpopular decisions. They were mocked, threatened, and arrested. But it is thanks to their sacrifice—and those of many other women— that women have the rights they have today.

THE CAST OF CHARACTERS

Alice Paul, women's rights activist (lived 1885 to 1977)

Elizabeth Cady Stanton, Abolitionist, social activist, & early suffragist (lived 1815 to 1902)

Susan B. Anthony, leader in early women's rights movement (lived 1820 to 1906)

Lucy Stone, early organizer for women's rights (lived 1818 to 1893)

World Antislavery Conference Organizer

Lucretia Mott, early Quaker minister, abolitionist and activist (lived 1793 to 1880)

Daniel Cady, Elizabeth Cady Stanton's father

Henry Stanton, Elizabeth Cady Stanton's husband

Martha Wright, younger sister of Lucretia Mott, served as a president of National Women's Rights Conventions (lived 1806 to 1875)

Lucy Burns, women's rights activist & close friend of Alice Paul; a founder of National Women's Party in 1916 (lived 1879 to 1966)

Inez Milholland, suffragist & labor lawyer (lived 1886 to 1916)

Woodrow Wilson, 28th U.S. President 1913-1921

Carrie Catt, suffrage leader, president of NAWSA, founder of League of Women Voters in 1920 (lived 1859 to 1947)

Joseph Tumulty, President Wilson's personal secretary

PROLOGUE

Old Alice Paul: What does voting mean to you?

Old Elizabeth Cady Stanton: Voting means I help choose who represents me.

Old Susan B. Anthony: I help make the laws.

Old Lucy Stone: My voice is as loud—and as powerful—as any man's!

Old E. C. Stanton: When I was a little girl, my father told me he wished I'd been born a boy.

Old L. Stone: My father was furious when I went to college.

Old S. B. Anthony: When I started to speak up, people called me a cackling hen.

Old E. C. Stanton: Men told me to go home and mind my children.

Old L. Stone: Newspapers said I was ugly. But when I spoke up, people heard me.

All women: People heard me.

Old A. Paul: This is the story of how American women found their voice. And how they fought for the right to use it.

Old E. C. Stanton: At first, people laughed at us.

Old L. Stone: They said it was selfish for us to demand rights.

Old S. B. Anthony: They told us to be patient.

Old A. Paul: The women who fought for women's **suffrage** didn't agree on everything.

Old S. B. Anthony: But we knew we deserved the same rights as any other citizen.

Old L. Stone: We deserved to own property.

Old S. B. Anthony: We deserved to go to college.

Old L. Stone: We deserved the freedom to speak up.

All: And we deserved the right to vote.

Old A. Paul: This is the story of women's suffrage.

ELIZABETH CADY STANTON

SUSAN B. ANTHONY

ALICE PAUL

SCENE ONE

July 1840
London, England

Old E. C. Stanton: In July 1840, hundreds of **abolitionists** travelled to London for the World Antislavery Convention. We were there to discuss how to end the horrible practice of slavery. My husband, Henry, and I were invited to attend. But I was having trouble getting through the door.

E. C. Stanton: What do you mean I can't come in?

Organizer: It's not that you can't come in. We're just deciding where to put you…

E. C. Stanton: Please put me with the rest of the **delegates**.

Organizer: Here in England it's not proper for men and women to sit together at a meeting.

Old E. C. Stanton: But soon enough, they found a solution.

Organizer: Right this way, Mrs. Stanton. We've found the perfect spot for you and the other ladies.

Old E. C. Stanton: I was led to a small room. A thick curtain separated it from the assembly room where the men sat. Soon, the five other women delegates joined me.

E. C. Stanton: But how can we be heard from here? How will we participate in the meeting?

Lucretia Mott: We won't. They don't want to hear what we have to say.

Old E. C. Stanton: So we sat there and listened to the men speak about slavery. And we agreed with every word. But we wondered: Who was speaking for the women? Women weren't free. We couldn't own property. We weren't considered equal to men. And we certainly couldn't vote. Who was fighting for our rights?

E. C. Stanton: How can these men talk about equality when we are treated like this?

Old E. C. Stanton: When the speeches were over, Lucretia Mott and I walked back to our hotels together. She was 27 years older than I was—and so much wiser.

L. Mott: You know, the men are afraid of what we have to say.

E. C. Stanton: What do you mean?

L. Mott: If they let us speak, they know we will soon begin fighting for our own rights.

E. C. Stanton: Imagine how the world would change if women were allowed to do what men can do.

Old E. C. Stanton: We decided to organize our own **conference** about women's rights. Back in the states, we met with people who shared our views. Not everyone agreed with us...

Dearest Lizzie,

I'm writing to ask you to stop speaking out for women's rights. Stop organizing this conference.

You say women should be able speak their minds, own property, and go to college. You even think women should vote! These are silly ideas. Don't you see when your husband votes, he votes for what is best for you?

Lizzie, please stop this nonsense. You are embarrassing your family.

Your father,

Daniel Cady

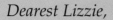

Old E. C. Stanton: Meanwhile, my husband, Henry, was not on my side either.

Henry Stanton: Lizzie, I need you at home to take care of our children while I am working.

E. C. Stanton: I do take care of our children. But can't you see how important this issue is to me—and to so many women?

H. Stanton: I've heard women say they don't even want to vote.

E. C. Stanton: Well then they don't have to!

Old E. C. Stanton: Lucretia and I planned the convention in my hometown of Seneca Falls, New York. In July 1848, I met with Lucretia and five other women to plan.

L. Mott: It will be a two-day conference.

Martha Wright: With several important speakers.

L. Mott: And Lizzie will give the main speech.

Old E. C. Stanton: I passed around a copy of the speech I had written. As they reached the end, their brows furrowed.

L. Mott: It's a perfect speech, Lizzie. Except for one thing. We can't demand the vote. Not now.

E. C. Stanton: You don't believe women should vote?

L. Mott: Of course I do. But Lizzie, we want people to take us seriously. If we ask for the vote now, we'll be laughed off the stage!

Old E. C. Stanton: I couldn't believe what Lucretia was saying. If we wanted a say in how the country was run, women had to vote. The time was now! So when I stepped onto the stage to give my speech, in front of about 300 people, I knew what to do. My speech began the same way as the Declaration of Independence.

E. C. Stanton: We hold these truths to be self-evident…

Old E. C. Stanton: But it included an important change.

E. C. Stanton: …that all men and *women* are created equal, that they have the right to life, **liberty**, and the pursuit of happiness….

Old E. C. Stanton: In 1776, our country's founders listed complaints about the King of England. So I listed the many ways women had been mistreated by men.

E. C. Stanton: Men have forced women to follow unfair rules. They have kept women from owning property. They have kept women in their homes…

Old E. C. Stanton: Then I read a list of demands—also called resolutions. The ninth resolution I spoke so loud, I hoped even the president could hear:

E. C. Stanton: *It is the duty of American women to fight for their right to vote in elections.*

Old E. C. Stanton: One hundred people—men and women—showed their support by signing the Seneca Falls Declaration. The next day, we were in the local newspaper.

Martha Wright: Lizzie, look. Your speech, The Declaration of Sentiments, is in the *New York Herald*.

E. C. Stanton: This is great news!

M. Wright: But the writer has mocked us. He even compared us to animals!

E. C. Stanton: That doesn't matter. If men and women read this, they will start thinking. That is the first step to any kind of change.

Old E. C. Stanton: And our declaration *did* get men and women thinking. Around the country, women began demanding rights.

L. Stone: Women want to be more than the limbs of society! We want to share with men all the happiness and sadness of human life!

Old E. C. Stanton: We knew that we had a cause worth fighting for. But we also knew we had a long fight ahead of us.

SCENE TWO

Old S. B. Anthony: Soon a women's movement had started. And Elizabeth Cady Stanton, Lucy Stone, and I were the leaders. Lizzie was the best writer, Lucy was the best speaker, and I was the main organizer. We became so close. We were like sisters.

1853
Boston, Massachusetts

Man: *(Opens door)* Can I help you?

S. B. Anthony: Good afternoon sir. We'd like to speak to you about our **petition** for women's rights.

Man: What kind of rights?

L. Stone: Well, sir, women are U.S. citizens the same way men are. We believe the U.S. Constitution gives us the same rights as men.

S. B. Anthony: With our petition, we hope to show your state government that people support women's rights.

Man: Get off my property! There's only one place for you women—at home!

Old S. B. Anthony: We were used to doors being slammed in our faces. We walked to the next house.

Woman: You knocked?

L. Stone: Hello there. We'd like to talk to you for a minute about your rights.

Woman: My husband doesn't like me talking to strangers.

Old S. B. Anthony: The woman was nervous. When we explained to her what we were doing, she started crying.

Woman: I support more freedom for women. But my husband doesn't. If he found out I signed a petition, I don't know what he'd do.

Old S. B. Anthony: We heard many stories like this. We hugged the woman and gave her our addresses.

S. B. Anthony: If you need anything, please write to us.

Old S. B. Anthony: We held annual women's rights conventions. Each year, the conventions grew bigger and better. But by 1860, people were more worried about war than about women. The northern and southern states disagreed on many issues, including slavery. And the South was threatening to **secede**. We discussed what we should do at the 1860 convention.

L. Stone: Ladies, everyone, even our supporters, think it's time we set aside our fight.

E. C. Stanton: I agree. Everyone knows a war is coming. We should spend our time supporting the north—and freedom for the slaves.

Old S. B. Anthony: I didn't want to stop, and I told them so.

E. C. Stanton: But Susan, you've been an abolitionist all your life.

S. B. Anthony: And I still am! But I don't want to wait a minute longer for *my* freedom than I need to.

L. Stone: But Susan, helping the slaves will help women.

E. C. Stanton: If a country can help one struggling group, it can help another.

Old S. B. Anthony: I was overruled. So we rallied our women to support the North. We gave speeches about freeing the slaves and giving them rights.

L. Stone: There can be no peace in this country until the people of African descent have the same rights as all American citizens!

Crowd: Hooray!

Old S. B. Anthony: …But sometimes we also demanded rights for women. That didn't always go over as well.

L. Stone: …And there can be no peace without equality for women!

Crowd: Get off the stage! Go home!

Old S. B. Anthony: We collected 400,000 signatures. Our hard work helped pass the 13th Amendment, which ended slavery, in 1865. Over the next few years, two amendments gave African Americans more rights. It was wonderful news. But there was one problem.

S. B. Anthony: The 15th Amendment says people cannot be denied the right to vote based on race or color.

E. C. Stanton: Race or color, but not sex?

S. B. Anthony: No!

E. C. Stanton: After all of our work, this is the thanks we get?

S. B. Anthony: I just can't believe it.

Old S. B. Anthony: We were furious. We hoped that when African Americans won their rights, so would women. We decided to fight even harder and never stop. We would focus on passing a **constitutional amendment** for women's suffrage. But Lucy disagreed.

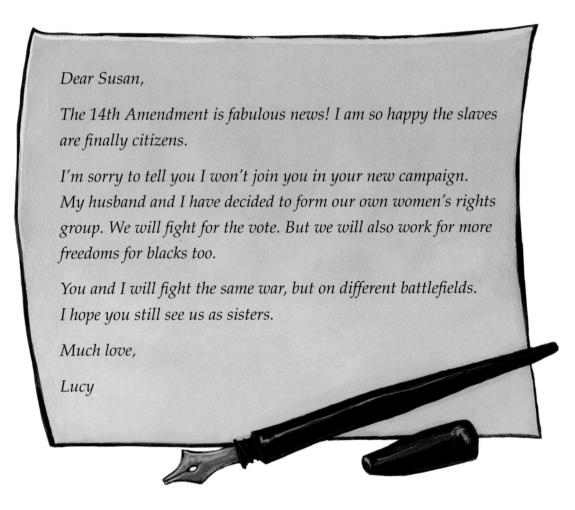

Dear Susan,

The 14th Amendment is fabulous news! I am so happy the slaves are finally citizens.

I'm sorry to tell you I won't join you in your new campaign. My husband and I have decided to form our own women's rights group. We will fight for the vote. But we will also work for more freedoms for blacks too.

You and I will fight the same war, but on different battlefields. I hope you still see us as sisters.

Much love,

Lucy

Old S. B. Anthony: Sadly, the women's movement split. Lizzie and I recruited thousands of women. We started a newspaper. In 1878, an amendment was proposed to Congress. It would have given women all the rights men had, but it was quickly voted down. We women still had work to do.

MEN'S LEAGUE FOR WOMEN'S

AMERICAN NURSES

VOTES FOR WOMEN

VOTE FOR WO...

DEMAND AN ...NDMENT TO T ...TITUTION OF ...TED STAT ...NCHISING WOMEN OF THIS C

Old A. Paul: By 1900, the lives of women had improved. More women than ever graduated from college. Many were working. But they still couldn't vote in national elections. I was ready to change that. Our **strategy** was to put pressure on the president.

March 2, 1913
Washington, D.C.

A. Paul: Now that Wilson is president, he must answer to the people!

Lucy Burns: We'll show him who the people are, won't we ladies?

Old A. Paul: Thousands of women gathered in Washington, DC to demand the right to vote. My fellow suffragists and I had organized a women's parade. Woodrow Wilson had recently been elected. The day before his **inauguration** we were ready to march!

Inez Millholland: You know, my sister thinks Wilson supports women's rights. She thinks he will give women the right to vote.

L. Burns: He gives many speeches about democracy and freedom.

A. Paul: Lots of politicians *talk* about democracy. I'm still waiting for the one that will fight for women's suffrage.

Old A. Paul: We started at the Capitol building. We marched down Pennsylvania Avenue, holding signs that read, "We Demand an Amendment to the Constitution Giving Women the Vote!" We sang "The Star Spangled Banner."

Women: *(singing)* O say can you see by the dawn's early light, What so proudly we hailed at the twilight's last gleaming.... .

L. Burns: What a crowd! How many people do you think there are?

A. Paul: Hundreds of thousands.

Old A. Paul: When we reached the Treasury Building, I spoke to a cheering crowd.

A. Paul: Votes for women! Say it with me!

Crowd: Votes for women!

Old A. Paul: It was a wonderful, peaceful parade. But as usual, there were angry protesters.

Angry man: Go home and cook dinner!

Angry woman: Who is minding the babies?

Old A. Paul: Soon, the protesters turned into a riot. Hundreds were hospitalized. The next day, women were banned from Wilson's inauguration parade. The newspapers claimed the riots were the fault of the women. Later that month, six women and I met with the president.

A. Paul: Thank you for meeting with us, Mr. President.

President Wilson: My pleasure. I must say you look so much more polite than I expected. Those were some nasty riots!

Old A. Paul: The president seemed happy to see us. But when we began to speak our minds, his mood changed.

L. Burns: Mr. President, I'd like to ask a question.

President Wilson: Go right ahead. Don't be nervous.

L. Burns: Well you see, Mr. President, I think we agree on most things.

President Wilson: Is that so?

L. Burns: Yes. In your book *The New Freedom*, you say the world is much different today than it was 20 years ago.

President Wilson: That's right.

A. Paul: Well, Mr. President, we agree with you. One thing that has changed is the confidence of American women. We are becoming more independent every day.

L. Burns: Women need the right to have a say in the direction of the country.

A. Paul: That's why it's time to pass the Susan B. Anthony Amendment, the amendment that gives women the right to vote.

Old A. Paul: The more we spoke, the more uncomfortable Wilson became.

President Wilson: Honestly, I have never considered women's suffrage. I will have to give it some thought. Thanks very much for coming. I must get back to work.

Old A. Paul: Each time we met with the president, he had another excuse.

President Wilson: Ladies, I'm busy trying to focus on other issues.

President Wilson: Ladies, the Democratic Party does not support it. I have to follow my party.

President Wilson: Ladies, please be patient.

I. Milholland: We have been waiting for 70 years!

A. Paul: This president will stall forever unless he is given a reason to move.

Ladies, the Democratic Party does not support it. I have to follow my party.

Ladies, please be patient.

Ladies, I'm busy trying to focus on other issues.

Old A. Paul: We organized parades, protests, and **picket lines**. We made billboards, wore pins and patches, and handed out our newspaper *The Suffragist.* Some people, even some suffrage supporters, thought we were being rude.

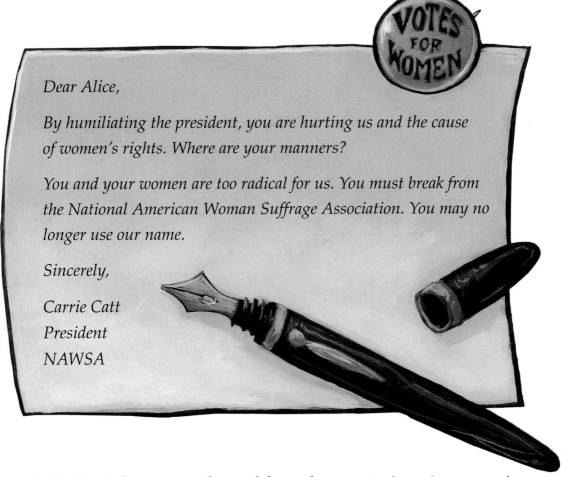

Dear Alice,

By humiliating the president, you are hurting us and the cause of women's rights. Where are your manners?

You and your women are too radical for us. You must break from the National American Woman Suffrage Association. You may no longer use our name.

Sincerely,

Carrie Catt
President
NAWSA

Old A. Paul: So we were booted from the country's main women's group, the NAWSA. We formed a new group, the National Women's Party. In January 1917, we began yet another protest outside the White House.

Joseph Tumulty: The women are protesting again, Mr. President.

President Wilson: So they are. How long have they been outside?

J. Tumulty: Three days, sir.

President Wilson: Three days?

J. Tumulty: That's right. Each day, they have stood from 10 to 5.

President Wilson: Have they been disturbing anyone?

J. Tumulty: No sir. They have just been standing silently with their signs.

Old A. Paul: We stood outside for weeks and weeks. One snowy day, the president's secretary invited us to warm up in the White House.

A. Paul: Tell the president we will come in only if he is ready to support the Susan B. Anthony Amendment.

Old A. Paul: By 1917, a war was raging in Europe. Wilson declared that the United States would send troops to defend our European friends. Like Anthony, Stone, and Stanton decades ago, we were told to stop our suffrage fight to support the war.

Dear Alice,

Your president is busy saving the free world. The NAWSA has stopped our suffrage work to support the war. If you know what's best for you and your country, you will do the same.

Carrie Catt
President
NAWSA

Old A. Paul: But we didn't stop. When foreign leaders visited the president, we protested louder. We wanted to let the world know America wasn't free.

A. Paul: America is not a democracy!

L. Burns: 20 million women are denied the right to vote!

I. Milholland: Our government must let its people speak before it will ever be free!

Old A. Paul: In June, the arrests started. We were thrown in a dirty prison without a trial. There we were treated worse than criminals. We started a **hunger strike**.

Police Officer: You're the fifth woman in here who didn't eat her lunch. What's wrong with you?

A. Paul: Until Wilson supports the Susan B. Anthony Amendment I won't eat a bite.

Police Officer: That ain't gonna happen, lady.

A. Paul: Then we won't need those meals, thank you.

Old A. Paul: News of our strike slowly spread. Many people didn't believe it—even the president.

J. Tumulty: Mr. President, what is the status of those suffragists in prison?

President Wilson: I'm not aware of any suffragists in prison.

J. Tumulty: There are reports of abuse. People say they are on a hunger strike.

President Wilson: You must be mistaken. We don't put people in prison for their political beliefs in this country.

Old A. Paul: When Wilson learned what was happening, we were quickly **pardoned** and released. Meanwhile, Wilson gave speeches about bringing peace and freedom to the world.

President Wilson: (*giving a speech*) What can come from this terrible war? We want to make the world safe for all people to live in. That means just and fair laws for all nations.

Old A. Paul: They were beautiful but empty words. So we went right back to protesting.

A. Paul: We demand suffrage now!

L. Burns: Our sons are overseas fighting for freedom, but where is that freedom at home?

I. Milholland: How long must women wait for liberty?

Old A. Paul: Even as Wilson ignored us, Congress took up our cause. The House of Representatives brought the suffrage amendment to a vote in 1918—and it passed! Eventually, Wilson realized what he had to do.

President Wilson: *(giving a speech)* The end of the Great War is near. The world is looking for our great democracy to lead them. If we reject laws like the women's suffrage amendment, the world may no longer believe in us.

Old A. Paul: I don't know if he supported women's suffrage in his heart. But it didn't matter. As he had said: the world was changing. The amendment was finally **ratified** by states in 1920. It was the exact same amendment written by Elizabeth Cady Stanton and Susan B. Anthony and presented to Congress 50 years before. Women across the country celebrated.

EPILOGUE

Old E. C. Stanton: But our fight wasn't over yet, was it?

Old A. Paul: No, It wasn't.

Old S. B. Anthony: There were still many laws that were unfair to women.

Old L. Stone: And there was still **discrimination** against women.

Old E. C. Stanton: Around the world today, many women can't vote.

Old A. Paul: In some places, women don't have the freedom to speak their views.

Old S. B. Anthony: Many women even face violence without **recourse**.

Old L. Stone: So it's up to future generations—to keep up the fight for liberty for all.

Old E. C. Stanton: To finish what we started.

WORDS TO KNOW

abolitionist: a person who supports officially ending slavery

conference: an official meeting in which people gather to talk about something

constitutional amendment: an official change to the U.S. Constitution that must be approved by two-thirds of both houses of Congress and three-fourths of the states

delegate: a person sent to speak for others at an event

discrimination: the unfair treatment of different categories of things or people

hunger strike: a type of protest in which a person refuses to eat until a change takes place

inauguration: a ceremony welcoming someone into office

liberty: freedom

pardon: to officially forgive a person, and not punish them, for a crime committed

petition: a written document that people sign to show their support for a change

picket line: a line or group of people protesting something

secede: to officially leave a religion, political party, country, or other group

strategy: a careful plan for reaching a goal

suffrage: the right to vote in elections

ratify: to make a law, treaty, or amendment official

recourse: a source of help

Learn More about Women's Suffrage

Books:

Bausum, Ann. *With Courage and Cloth: Winning the Fight for a Woman's Right to Vote.* National Geopgraphic Children's Books, 2005.

Kamma, Anne. *If You Lived When Women Won Their Rights.* Scholastic, 2008 edition.

Wallner, Alexandra. *Susan B. Anthony.* Holiday House, 2012.

Web Sites:

Woman Suffrage biographies: https://www.nwhm.org/education-resources/biography/woman-suffrage

Women's Rights National Park Resources: http://www.nps.gov/wori/index.htm

Places

The Carrie Chapman Catt Home and Museum, Charles City, Iowa.

The National Women's History Museum, Washington, DC.

The Susan B. Anthony House, national landmark home and headquarters, Rochester, New York.

Women's Rights National Park & Museum, Seneca Falls, New York.